# AUSTINATO

An Ostinato Jamboree
for
Voices and Orff Instruments

by

## Konnie Saliba

Michael D. Bennett, Editor

Darva Campbell, Artist

ISBN 0-934017-25-5

## Memphis Musicraft Publications

4096 Blue Cedar • Lakeland, TN 38002

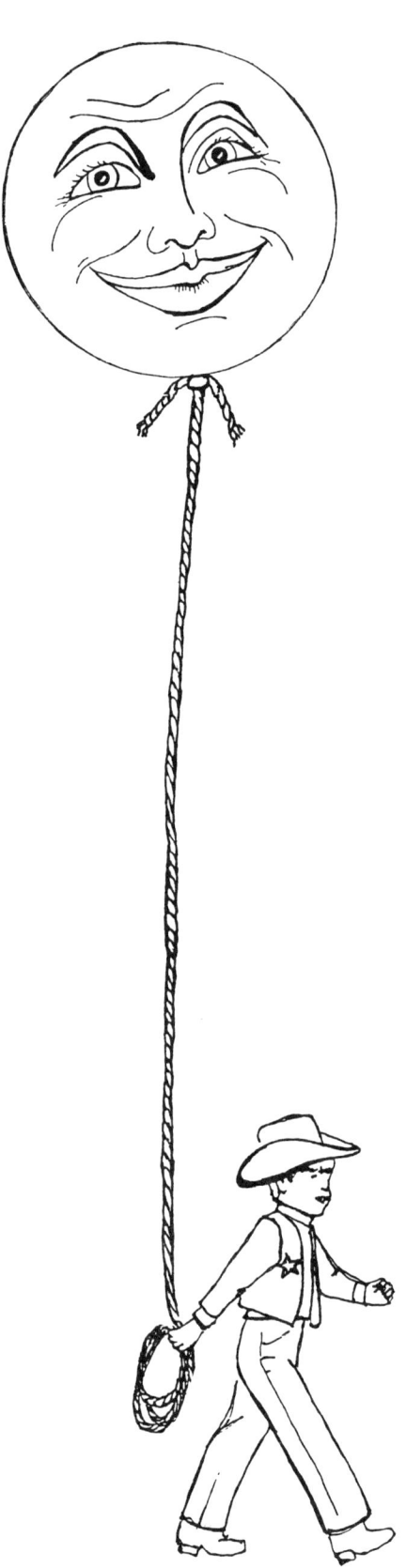

© Copyright 1996
**Memphis Musicraft Publications**

All rights reserved. No part of this publication may be reproduced or distributed in any form without the written consent of the publisher.

# CONTENTS

**Instrument Guide** . . . . . . . . . . . iii

**Preface** . . . . . . . . . . . iv

**Speech Ostinatos**
- *Obstinato* . . . . . . . . . . . 1
- *Ladles & Jelly Spoons* . . . . . . . . . . 2

**Body Percussion Ostinatos**
- *Bubblegum* . . . . . . . . . . . 3
- *Put on Stamps* . . . . . . . . . . 4
- *Peter Meter* . . . . . . . . . . . 6

**Unpitched Percussion Ostinatos**
- *D-R-U-M-S* . . . . . . . . . . . 8
- *Six Drums Over Texas* . . . . . . . . . 10
- *Burple, Burple Boo* . . . . . . . . . . 11
- *Listen to the Drums* . . . . . . . . . . 12

**Barred Instrument Ostinatos**
- *Music Starts Our Day* . . . . . . . . . 13
- *Catch Me* . . . . . . . . . . . 14
- *I Think I'm in Love with Borduns* . . . . . . . 15
- *Can You Peel a Glockenspiel?* . . . . . . . . 16
- *Hey, Mr. Xylophone* . . . . . . . . . . 17
- *G, Can You Spell?* . . . . . . . . . . 18
- *Oh, Say Can You C?* . . . . . . . . . . 20
- *Dawn* . . . . . . . . . . . 21

**Barred & Unpitched Instrument Ostinatos**
- *Little Green Frog* . . . . . . . . . . 22
- *Gertie Sue* . . . . . . . . . . . 24
- *Ride the Carousel* . . . . . . . . . . 26
- *What Time Is It?* . . . . . . . . . . 27
- *Konnie's Music Students* . . . . . . . . . 28
- *Fred Pentatonic* . . . . . . . . . . 30

**Vocal & Unpitched Instrument Ostinatos**
- *Austinato* . . . . . . . . . . . 32
- *If You Like Me* . . . . . . . . . . 33
- *Hot Dog* . . . . . . . . . . . 34

# INSTRUMENT GUIDE

## DRUMS & UNPITCHED PERCUSSION

| | | | |
|---|---|---|---|
| ⊖ | bass drum | | piccolo blocks |
| ○○ | bongo drums | | sleigh bells |
| | brass chime bars | | slit drum |
| | cabasa | | snare drum |
| | claves | | suspended cymbal |
| | conga drum | | tambourine |
| | cowbell | | temple blocks |
| | guiro | | timpani |
| ○ | hand drum | △ | triangle |
| | log drum | | vibraslap |
| | maracas | | wood block |

## BARRED INSTRUMENTS

- SG    soprano glockenspiel
- AG    alto glockenspiel
- SM    soprano metallophone
- AM    alto metallophone
- BM    bass metallophone
- SX    soprano xylophone
- AX    alto xylophone
- BX    bass xylophone
- CBX    contra bass bar

## BODY PERCUSSION

- Cl    clap
- Pt    pat knee
- Sn    snap
- St    stamp

## OTHER

- Gt    guitar
- Per    all previous percussion
- V    voices

# PREFACE

Ostinato is derived from the Latin word *ostinatus*—stubborn. In music, ostinato is an elemental structural device which persistently repeats a pattern or motive. For an Orff Schulwerk teacher, ostinato is perhaps the most useful tool we have since it can be used verbally, bodily, instrumentally, vocally, and in movement. Ostinato patterns can be devised to appropriately challenge the most limited and the most talented students, then become integrated parts of a simple or complex musical composition. Ostinato is the bridging device which leads students through rounds and canons to independent part performance.

Ostinato is also a most effective classroom management tool. Every child in the room can be involved simultaneously in different tasks— listening, coordinating body movement, developing rhythmic accuracy or improving performance technique skills. There is no time for trouble!

Teachers ask me when they should begin teaching ostinato. When children have sufficient skill to perform body percussion phrase patterns, it is time for the challenge of ostinato. This usually takes place in the second grade. Prior to this, children need to perform pulse patterns as accompaniments. (On-the-beat pat, clap, pat, clap, for example.) When children are competent with various body percussion pulse patterns they are ready for ostinato.

I begin with speech ostinatos, followed by short text phrases used to accompany a song or story. Next come body percussion, unpitched percussion, barred instruments, and finally vocal ostinatos. Movement ostinatos can be used with both speech and song to precede structured dance movement.

It is important for all ostinatos to have a good rhythmic structure. The pattern should have rhythmic variety with tension and relaxation. Two to four measures will be the typical length. Don't forget to vary the meter. Rhythm ostinatos should complement, not copy, the rhythm they accompany. Pitched ostinatos should complement, not copy, the melody they accompany. Using complementary motives within an ostinato will help prepare students for question-answer rhythmic and melodic phrases.

**AUSTINATO** demonstrates my ideas on ostinato with twists of humor, parody and silly fun. (The dust devil made me do it!) My objective is to show how ostinato can be a vital tool for teaching anything and everything. The activities are arranged in order of difficulty within each ostinato type so you can quickly find the models you need. Additional ostinato possibilities are given as lesson extensions at the end of most activities.

Let this most flexible of tools be your constant helper, as it is mine.

Konnie Saliba
Memphis, TN

# OBSTINATO

**Speech Ostinatos**  Konnie Saliba

All: Os - ti - na - tos are ob - sti - nant. We use them as ac - com - p'ni - ments.

O-1: I am ve - ry stub - born.

O-2: *low voice* Ob - sti - nant  *high voice* os - ti - na - to.

O-3: Let's add a new one, one that is hip and jazz - y.

All: First, clap the rhy - thm of this lit - tle rhyme. Then add the os - ti - na - tos one at a time.

## Process Suggestions
- Speak the rhyme for the class then teach it to them. Use a visual to aid comprehension.
- Divide the class; half speak the rhyme, half speak ostinato 1. Show voice levels.
- Divide class into three parts and speak only the ostinatos.
- Make further divisions and perform any two, then three ostinatos with the rhyme.

## Extensions
- Transfer the rhythm of the rhyme to claps, ostinato 1 to stamps, ostinato 2 to snaps, ostinato 3 to knee pats. Speak the rhyme with these body percussion.
- Transfer the ostinatos to unpitched percussion of your choice. Add these to the rhyme.
- Have students create additional ostinatos.

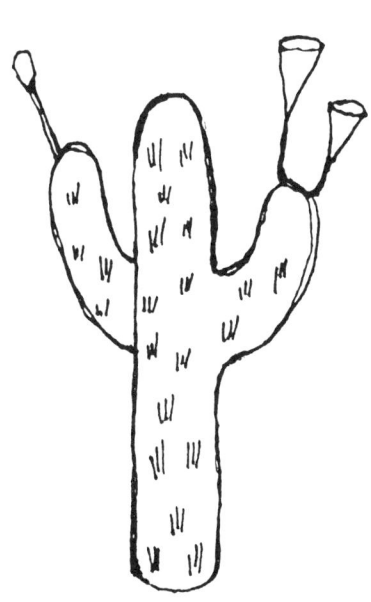

# LADLES AND JELLY SPOONS

**Speech Ostinato**  arr. Konnie Saliba

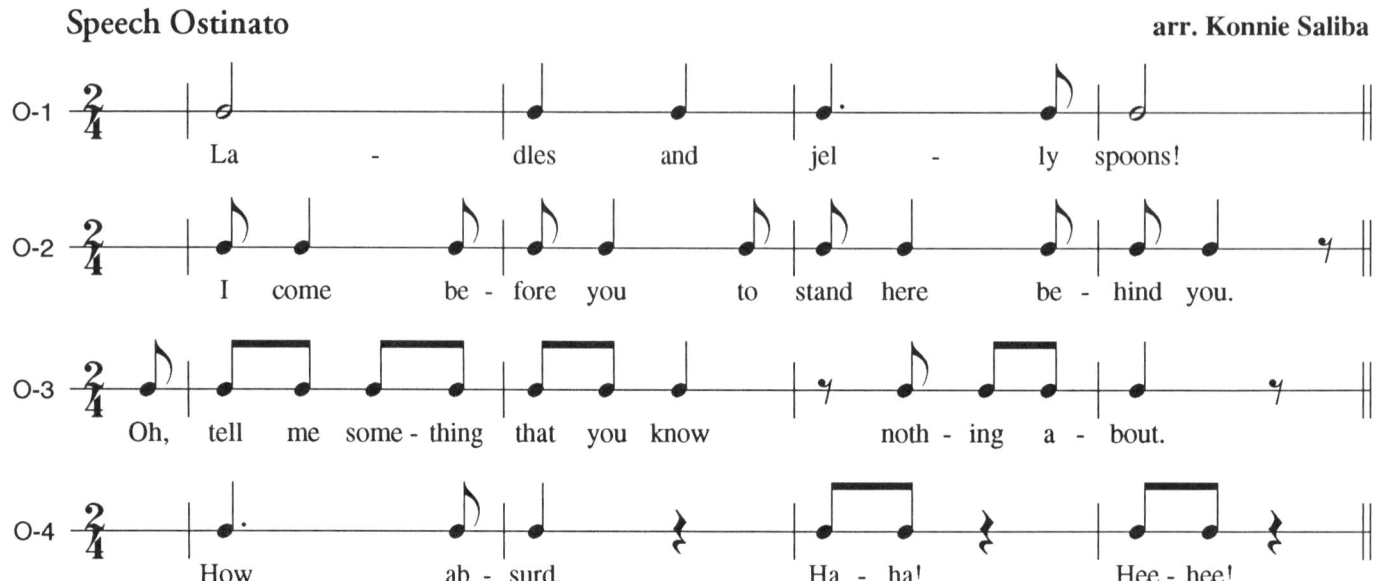

O-1: La - dles and jel - ly spoons!
O-2: I come be - fore you to stand here be - hind you.
O-3: Oh, tell me some - thing that you know noth - ing a - bout.
O-4: How ab - surd. Ha - ha! Hee - hee!

## Process Suggestions

- Teach the four ostinatos to all students as separate patterns.
- Divide into four groups, each responsible for one pattern. Point to groups in sequence to perform the verse.
- Point to groups in random order to perform just their segment two or three times. Each group stops when a new one enters.
- Point to groups in random order. This time they keep repeating their ostinato as you add one or two or three other ostinatos. You may signal any group out so that at any given time there will be 2, 3, or 4 ostinatos going. End with ostinato 4.
- Rotate the ostinato assignments.
- Let a student be the director and repeat.

## Extensions

- Transfer each ostinato pattern to an unpitched percussion instrument. Perform as an instrumental piece or an instrumental/speech piece.
- Perform the verse as a four-part canon with entrances every four measures. Each group begins with part 1 and speaks the entire verse. (Delete the eighth-rest at the end of part 2 and change the eighth-rest to a quarter-rest at the end of part 3.) Begin *pp* and end *F.*

# BUBBLEGUM

**Body Percussion Pulse Patterns**

**Konnie Saliba**

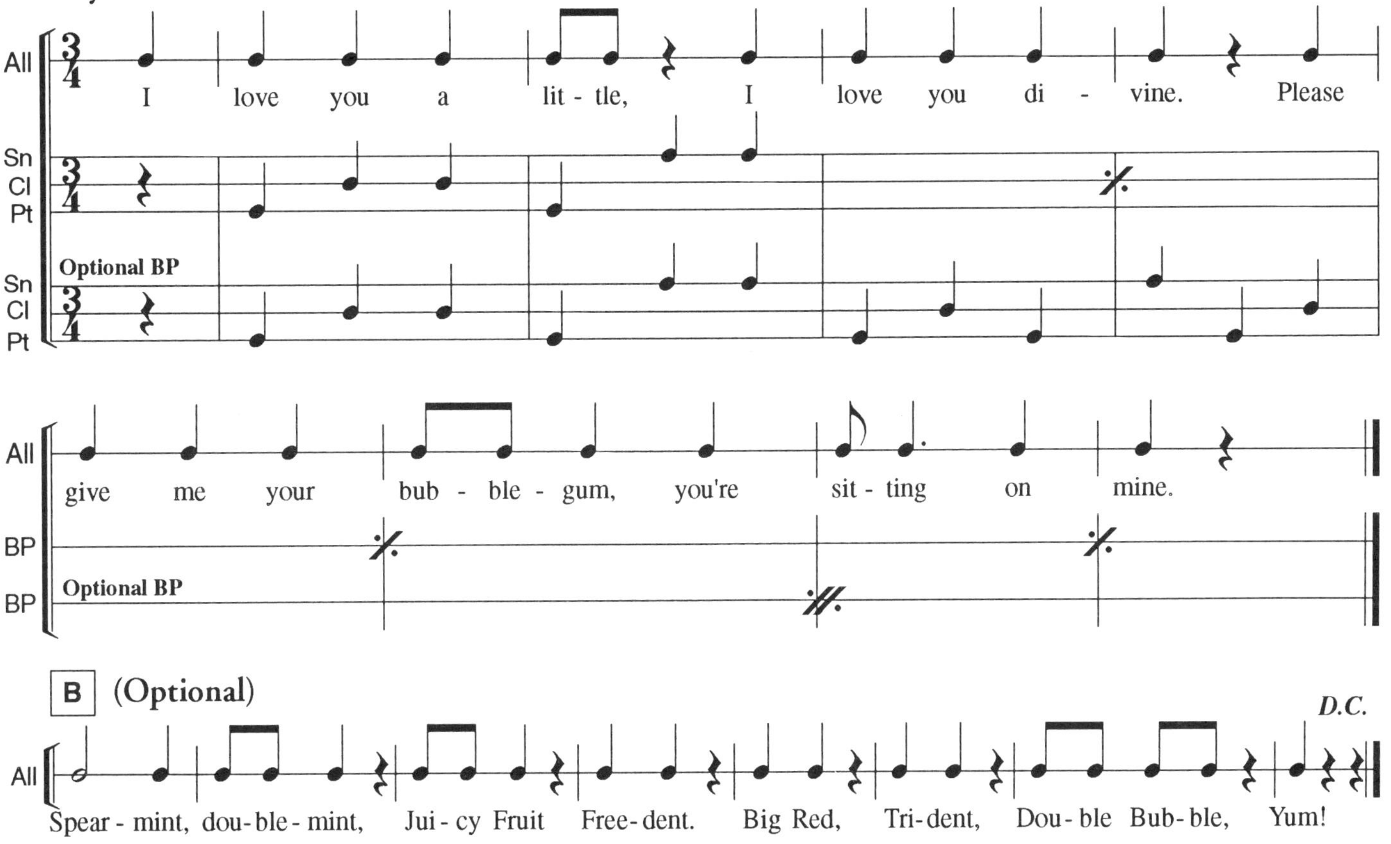
All
I love you a lit - tle, I love you di - vine. Please
Sn
Cl
Pt
Optional BP
give me your bub - ble - gum, you're sit - ting on mine.
BP
Optional BP
B
(Optional)
D.C.
Spear - mint, dou - ble - mint, Jui - cy Fruit Free - dent. Big Red, Tri - dent, Dou - ble Bub - ble, Yum!

## Rhyme Process Suggestions

- Teach the triple meter rhyme to the class.
- Add the BP pulse pattern of your choice.

## Extensions

- Add the gum word B section (no pulse pattern) with a *D.C.*
- Have students create other BP pulse patterns.
- Have students create a different B section with new gum names.

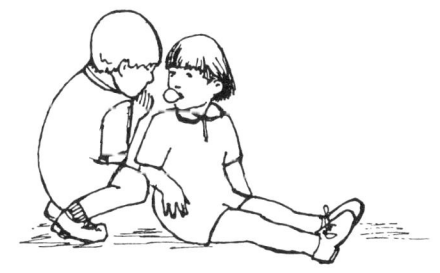

# BUBBLEGUM

**Body Percussion Ostinato**

**Konnie Saliba**

V
I love you a lit - tle, I love you di - vine.
Sn
Cl
Pt

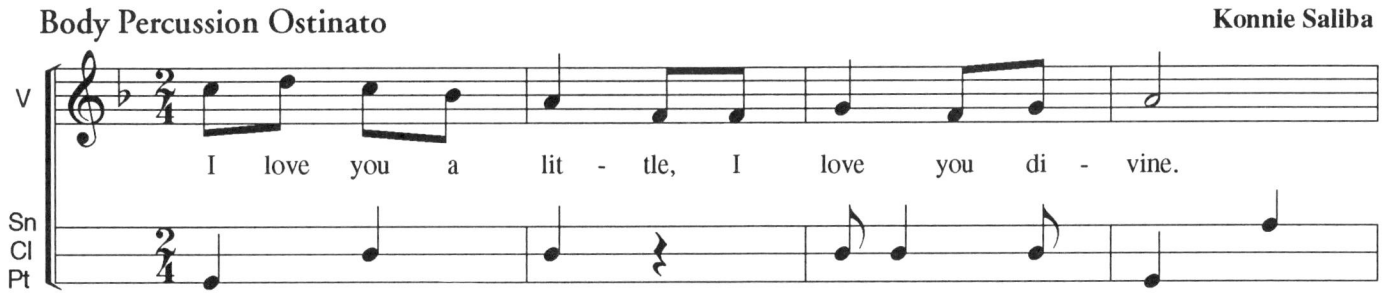

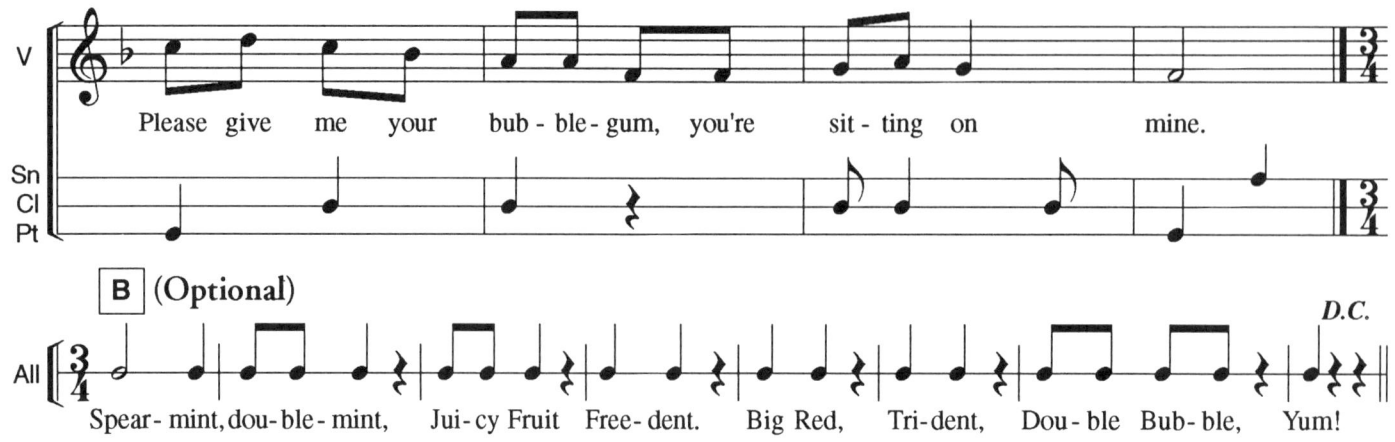

### Melody Process Suggestions
- Teach the duple meter melody to the class. (This could be another speech-only rhythm.)
- Add the ostinato.

### Extensions
- Add the gum word B section (no ostinato) with a *D.C.*
- Have students create a different B section using their favorite gum names.
- Have students create other ostinatos.
- Perform the two *Bubblegums* in series. To help students make the metric transition, play a 4-bar improvisation in-between versions using the next meter.

# PUT ON STAMPS

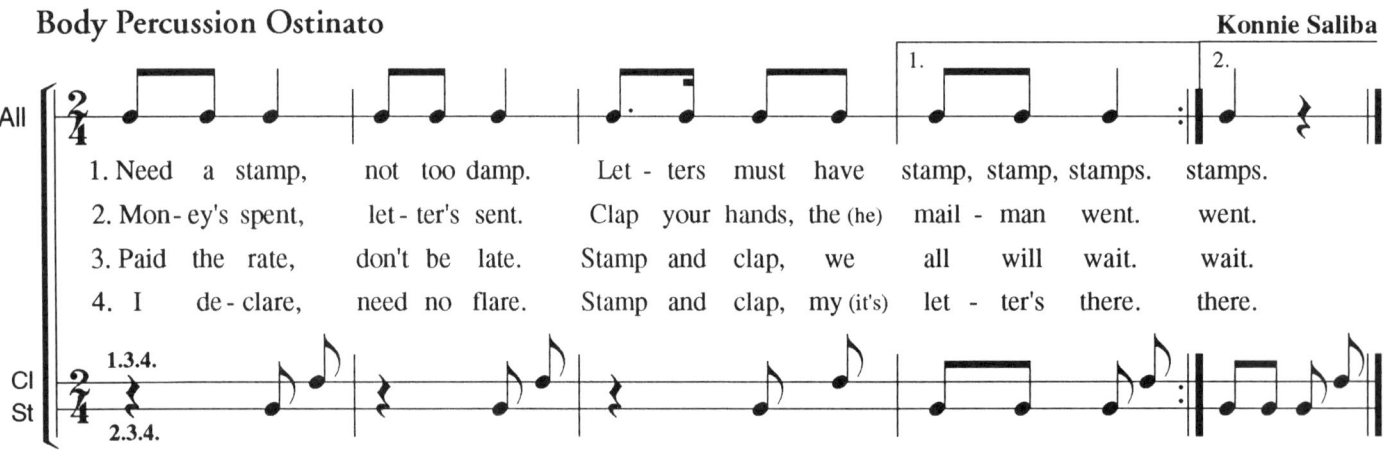

### Process Suggestion
- Divide class. Group 1 speaks, group 2 performs BP as indicated. Omit the stamp in verse 1 and the clap in verse 2. Use the words in parentheses on the repeat of lines 2 and 4. Switch groups.

### Extension
- To demonstrate how you can expand from a simple rhyme with BP ostinato, we have added a melody to this rhyme. It can be sung as a 12-bar song with ostinato, or in canon. We have used the same ostinato, but feel free to be original.

# PUT ON STAMPS

Konnie Saliba

**Body Percussion Ostinato**

[Musical notation with three phrases]

Phrase 1 (V/St): Need a stamp, not too damp. Let-ters must have stamp, stamp, stamps. stamps.

Phrase 2 (V/Cl): Mon-ey's spent, let-ter's sent. Clap your hands, the (he) mail-man went. went.

Phrase 3 (V/Cl/St):
Paid the rate, don't be late. Stamp and clap, while we all wait.
I de-clare, need no flare. Stamp and clap, my let-ter's there.

## Process Suggestions

- Teach each four-bar melodic phrase to everyone. Have students perform BP as they sing each phrase.
- Divide into three groups. Each sings its own phrase (no BP). Perform *Stamps* in additive fashion (1, 1+2, 1+2+3). You may perform the song in add/substract fashion too. (1, 1+2, 1+2+3, 2+3, 3). Note that on the repeat of phrase 3, different lyrics are sung.
- Repeat. Add BP this time.

## Extensions

- Sing the song as a true canon. Each group sings the entire song.
- Ask students to devise a new BP ostinato, choosing from snaps, pats, claps or stamps. The lyrics could also be changed.

# PETER METER

**Variation 4** *Slowly*

Poor Peter Meter. Sad Peter Meter. Lost his fair wife in six-eight meter.
Put her in a tempo slow, and for six beats she wanders to-and-fro.

*Faster*

But when the tempo skips so fast, the six become two. He found her at last.
Put her in a six-eight pumpkin. Compound meter, lots of jumpin'.

# Author's Note

- This activity demonstrates four of the innumerable ways a simple verse can be used to introduce different meters. We have varied the difficulty of the rhythm and the BP ostinato in each variation to show how you could adapt this kind of lesson to any skill level.
- Compound meters (6/8, 9/8, 12/8, 6/4) are not as commonly used as simple meters. It is not easy to explain the dual roles of compound meter to young musicians. We hope Peter helps demonstrate the difference.
- Speak the traditional rhyme if you would like a theme to precede the variations.

# Process Suggestion

- Separately, teach each rhyme to the class.
- Add the BP ostinato to the rhyme.
- Perform the four variations in series.
  Use a four-bar BP intro/interlude before each variation.

# Extension

- Students create new rhythm patterns for each meter's rhyme.
- Create new BP ostinatos.

## Process Suggestions

- Teach the song to the class. If the students know the song, *B-I-N-G-O,* begin with this.
- Teach the new lyrics using a visual.
- Select the drum/drums you wish to play in measures 6-13. You may want to use a soloist, a group of like drums or a different drum for each of the five notes.
- Sing/play the A section with guitar.
- Prepare the speech B section with a visual.
- Add the timpani ostinato.
- Perform sections A and B.
- Let students help determine how section C should be performed (soloist, group, Q/A).
- Perform the entire first verse.
- For verses 2 and 3, select woods, then metals for the A section to replace the drums.
- Substitute a BX, then a BM for the timpani ostinato.
- In the section B lyrics, change "drums" to "woods" or "metals" in verses 2 and 3.

# SIX DRUMS OVER TEXAS

arr. Konnie Saliba

## Process Suggestions
- Teach the song to the class. If the students know *Have You Ever Seen a Lassie,* begin there.
- Show the new lyrics on a visual. The instrument name changes in each verse: 1. bass drum 2. snare drum 3. conga drum 4. slit drum 5. hand drum 6. bongo drum. Each instrument plays its name ostinato in ms. 2-4. Accompany on guitar. Do not repeat section A on the *D.C.*
- In section B the featured instrument plays a new ostinato. (Section B is not additive.)
- After all six verses have been played/sung go to the additive coda. Beginning with the bass drum, instruments add their section B ostinatos. Additive segments may be four or eight measures long.

## Extension
- Invite students to create different ostinatos for the instruments.
- Use the coda for a free improvisation by the featured instruments.

# BURPLE, BURPLE BOO

**Unpitched Ostinatos**

Konnie Saliba

Che che che che che che che che che che che che che che choo!

Yuk!  Yuk,

Cla - ves sound hap - py!

Tem - ple blocks are tons of fun to play!

Wood block. Wood block. *Now he's sick, he's 8 beats si - lent!* (whisper loudly)

Gui - ro. Gui - ro It's a weird-o, weird-o sound, weird-o, weird-o sound.

Bur - ple, bur - ple boo, the slit drum.

## Process Suggestions

- Teach the rhythm for each ostinato using only the text phrases. Note that some patterns may be more easily learned in pairs (vibraslap/claves and guiro/wood block, for example).
- Transfer rhythms to the instruments and perform in additive form (bottom up). Use four or eight-bar statements for each instrument.

## Extensions

- Use 8 measure statements. For each new entrance, have students speak the text phrase along with the instrument for four measures, then instrument only for four measures.
- Have students create new text phrases for each instrument.
- For variety, use top down additive form.
- Use this piece as a model for new student compositions.

# LISTEN TO THE DRUMS

## Author's Note

*Listen to the Drums* demonstrates a more complex use of ostinato technique which will musically challenge more advanced students. Section A uses layered ostinatos of varying length and dynamics. Section B uses alternating phrase ostinatos and layering. The B section will also challenge students with its asymmetric conga accents and rapid bongo pattern.

## Process Suggestions

- Teach the rhythm for each ostinato using only the text phrases. Transfer the patterns to BP, then to the drums. Use the hand drum 2 ostinato as a helper for teaching the hand drum 3 ostinato.
- Spoken phrases may be added to the initial statement of each ostinato during performance.
- Do not repeat section A on the *D.C.*

# MUSIC STARTS OUR DAY

Konnie Saliba

**Barred Instrument Ostinato**

Lyrics: Let us sing and dance and play. Mu-sic to start and end the day.
We will sing and we will play and dance our way. Mu-sic to start and end the day.

## Process Suggestions
- Teach the melody to the class by rote.
- Sing the melody as a two-part canon. Switch parts.
- Add the barred instrument ostinato.
- Sing the melody as a three, then a four-part canon if your students are ready.

## Extension
- Sing the melody in unison with accompaniment as section A. Add a 16-measure B section for improvisation by selected students on unpitched percussion instruments. Repeat A.
- Use the above B section with canonic A sections.

# CATCH ME

## Process Suggestions
- Teach the unison melody. Begin with text in rhythm, then perform as a speech canon.
- When students are secure, divide into two groups and perform as a canon. Switch parts.
- Add the bordun accompaniment and perform.
- Set up the other barred instruments in d minor pentatonic. Have students play the melody in unison using just finger nails. Transfer to mallets.
- Perform the canon instrumentally. You may make the form longer by using sung/played canons.

## Extensions
- Teach the alternate accompaniment and perform *Catch Me* as a unison song.
- To really challenge students, perform the canon at a one bar interval.

# I THINK I'M IN LOVE WITH BORDUNS

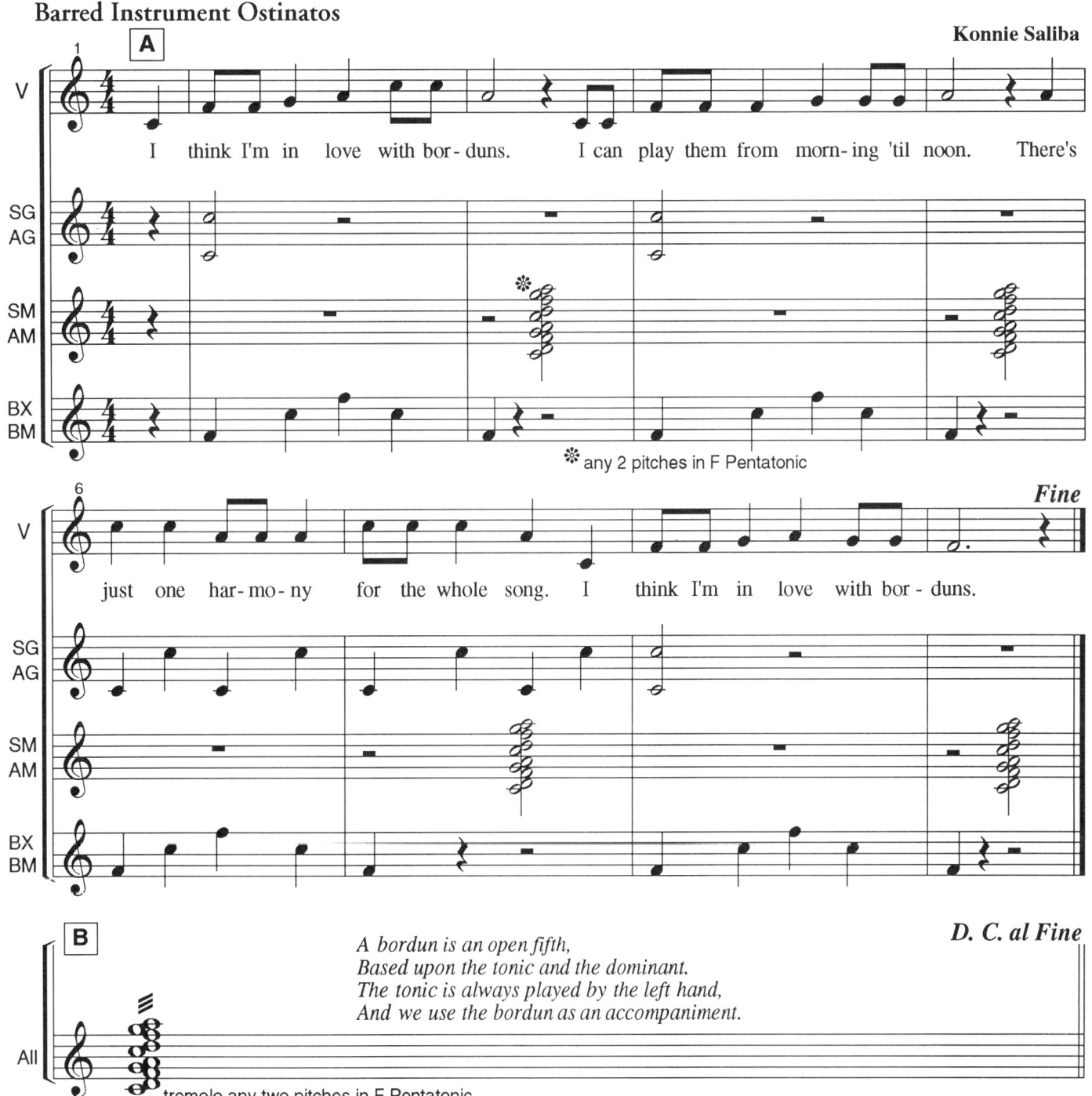

## Process Suggestions
- Prepare the song, then the accompaniment.
- The B section serves as a style contrast to A and also as a bordun tutor. An interesting way to perform B is for the class to echo your speech a line at a time.

## Extension
- Demonstrate each line in section B with speech and an instrument. Class echoes your demonstration of each line.

# CAN YOU PEEL A GLOCKENSPIEL?

**Barred Instrument Ostinato**

arr. Konnie Saliba

*(Lyrics:)* You can peel a ba-na-na, that's no big deal. You can peel a po-ta-to and an on-ion too. You can peel an ap-ple and make a meal. But you nev-er can peel a glock-en-spiel.

## Process Suggestions
- Make a visual of the lyrics with special words underlined.
- Teach the song, then the ostinato, to the class.
- Ask for suggestions for unpitched instruments (or home made sounds) to use with each special word.
- Sing the song; sing and play the special words.
- Sing the song except for the special words; play them.

## Extension
- Play the accompaniment and special word instruments only; no singing.

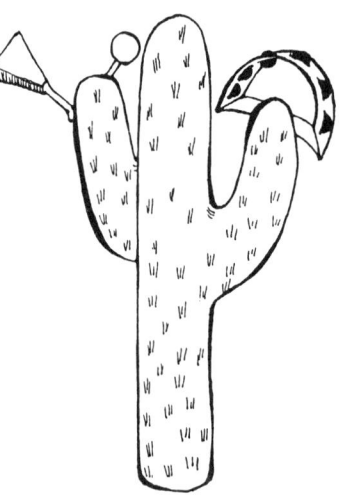

# HEY, MR. XYLOPHONE

**Barred Instrument Ostinatos**

Konnie Saliba

[Sheet music: Section A, measures 1-8, with parts for V (voice), SG/SM AG/AM, SX AX, and BX BM. Lyrics: "Hey, Mister Xy-lo-phone, Xy-lo-pone, Xy-lo-phone. Hey, Mister Xy-lo-phone. Play a song for me." Fine at measure 8.]

[Section B, measure 9: 8 measure improvisation, D.C. al Fine]

## Process Suggestions
- Teach the melody, then the ostinatos, to the class.
- All xylophones play a C Pentatonic improvisation in section B.
- Add verses for other mallet groups. (Ms Glockenspiel, for example.)

## Extensions
- Have only one type instrument play the improvisation—alto xylophones, for example.
- Choose a pair of students to play a Q/A improvisation in section B.

17

## Process Suggestions

### Section A
- Teach the melody to the class. Use a visual of the G Pentatonic scale to help.
- Add SG/AG to the vocal motive.
- Add the bass/alto bordun.
- Perform section A.

### Section B
- Ask students to combine the letter names from the scale to form words. There are numerous ways to perform the B section. Choose a method that fits students' abilities. Two suggestions:
    1. Student spells a word, class says the word; repeat the sequence.
    2. Student spells a word; student (same or others) plays the word on an instrument; class echo-sings the pitches; class says the word.

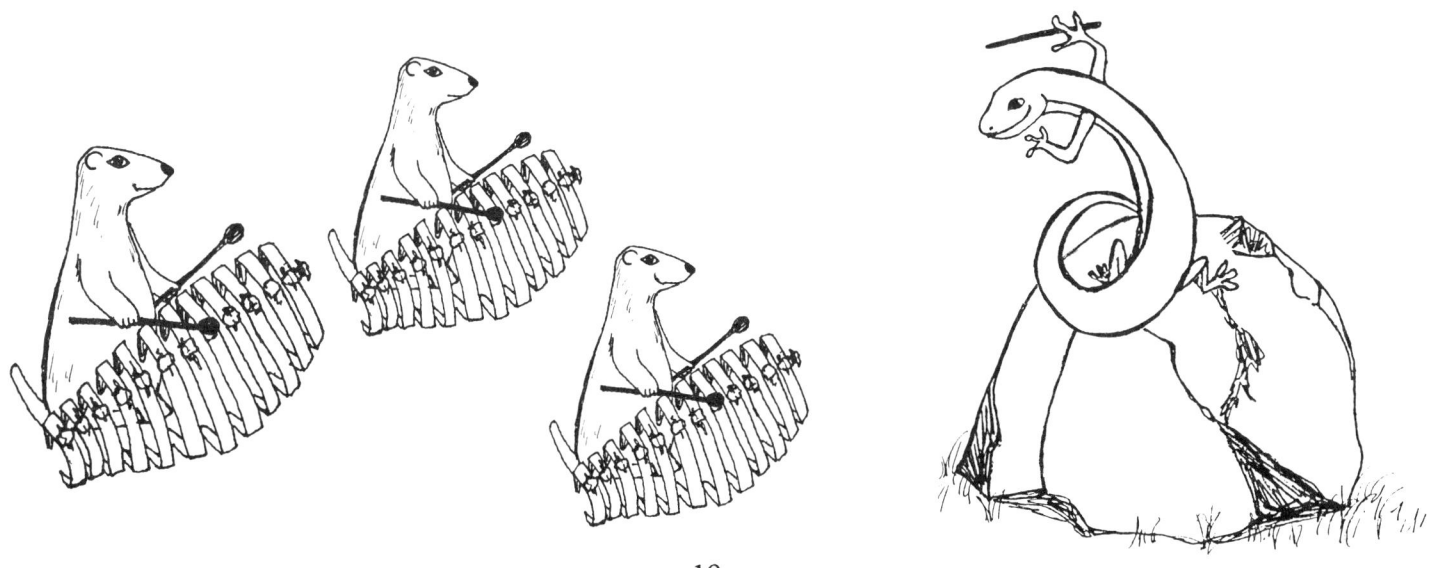

# OH, SAY CAN YOU C?

**Barred Instrument Ostinatos**

Konnie Saliba

*any two pitches in C Pentatonic

## Author's Note
For the benefit of expressive variety, we have modified the classic requirement that an ostinato repeat regularly. This will not be the only time we take a few liberties! (Don't let technical requirements get in the way of musicality in your work.)

## Process Suggestions
- Teach the melody to the class.
- Teach the mallet ostinatos and add to the melody.
- Repeat the two-bar spoken part in *Old MacDonald* additive fashion through the four verses.
- Add one mallet ostinato per verse. (Suggest BX/BM, SG/AG, SM/AM in verses 2, 3, and 4.).

## Extensions
- Have students sing pitch letter names in ms. 7-8 to reinforce awareness of pitch names.
- Ask students to devise new pairs of F-B words to use in ms. 5-6; the more absurd, the better.
- Transfer all the F-B words to various unpitched instruments for even more fun.

# DAWN

**Barred Instrument Ostinatos**

Konnie Saliba

*[Musical score: Intro/Coda section with SM and AM parts in 4/4, marked pp cresc. to mf, ending with Fine]*

*[Musical score: Verse section marked D.C. al Fine, with V/SM, SG/AG, AM, BX/BM, brass chimes glissando, and CBX parts]*

Lyrics: Ring like bells, deep in the night. Bring-ing the day and the dawn of light.

("any two pitches" marking on AM part)

## Author's Note

Have students help design the dynamic stage for this brief but expressive piece. Effective dynamic accompaniment will make a big difference.

## Process Suggestions

- Teach students the melody.
- Add the SM to the melody. (Voices drop out and SM plays the melody on the repeat.)
- Add the four ostinato lines from section A.
- Prepare the intro/coda. Use two players per part, each using two mallets.

## Extension

- Ask students to revise the lyrics and accompaniment to reflect the end of day: setting sun, cool night, stars, night sounds.
- Have a few students speak the verse over the accompaniment.

# LITTLE GREEN FROG

## Process Suggestions

- Prepare the song and the ostinatos.
- Give students a chance to suggest different instruments for the A section unpitched ostinato.
- Add the section rhythmic speech, then the ostinato.

## Extension

- Students make-up another speech-rhythm story for section B.
- Students create another unpitched ostinato to accompany section B.

# GERTIE SUE

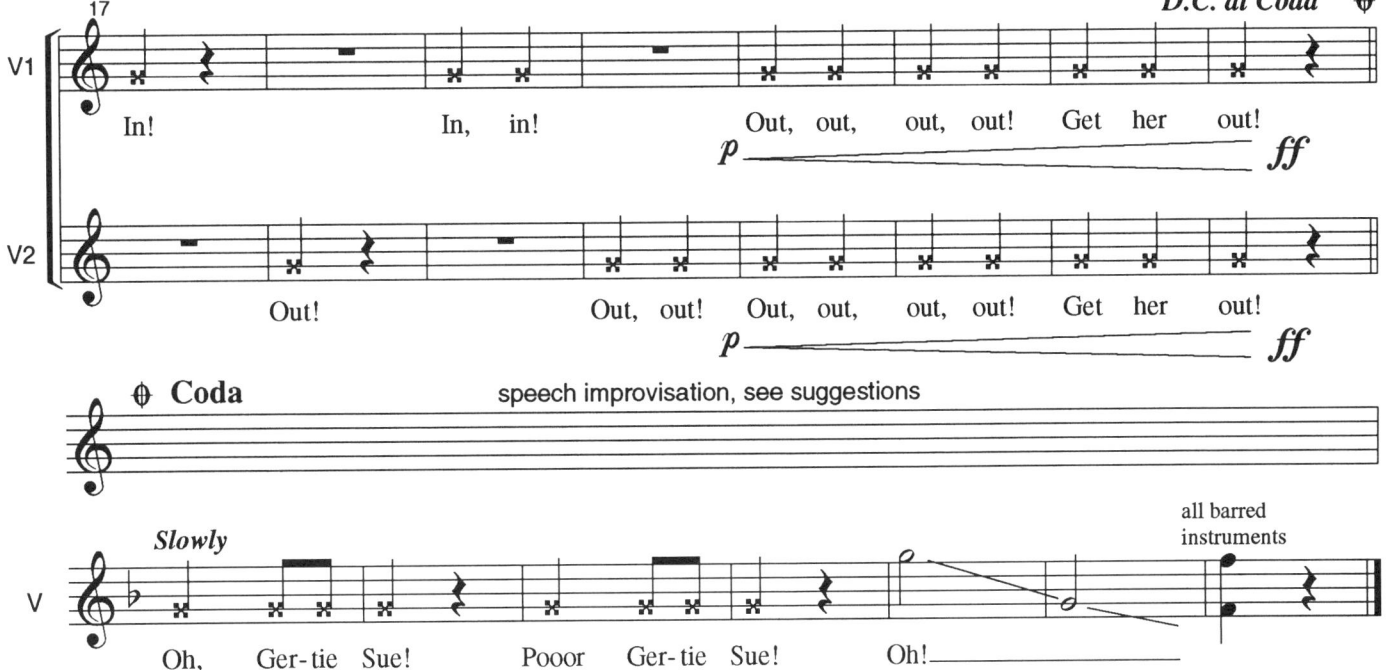

## Process Suggestions

- Teach the song to the class.
- Add the ostinatos and perform section A.
- Divide class into two groups (boys/girls, left/right) and teach the spoken B section. Encourage expressive feelings!
- In performance, repeat sections A and B, then proceed to the coda.
- In the coda, each student turns to a neighbor and vividly projects the plight of poor Gertie Sue. For example, "It's cold in the water." The fish will bite her nose!" "Can she swim?" "I bet she's scared," and so forth. This is an opportunity for verbal expression with high voices, low voices, excitement, and drama. Let the hubbub continue for 30 seconds or so and then slowly close your hands, signaling the end of the section.
- Without a break, conduct the final phrase in a slow, rubato tempo. All barred instruments play octave Fs at the end.

# RIDE THE CAROUSEL

## Process Suggestions
- Teach the vocal melody to the class.
- Prepare the accompaniment: basses and AM for first time, AX and sleigh bells for second time.
- Prepare the SG and AG melody/countermelody parts.
- Perform the piece two times with the following orchestration:
    - A:  voices on melody with basses and AM bordun.
    - A1: SG melody, AG countermelody with AX and sleigh bells ostinatos.

# WHAT TIME IS IT?

**Barred & Unpitched Instrument Ostinatos**

arr. Konnie Saliba

## Author's Note

If you have never taught a 12/8 piece, try this. Teach the melody as if it were in 4/4 with AG triplets. Write the music on the board in 4/4. Tell students there is another way to write these same sounds, feeling three subdivisions of the beat, without using triplets. Write the example in 12/8 and play it.

## Process Suggestions

- Teach all metal players the melody in a whole-note, non-metered fashion. These players practice the melody in each meter.
- Add the AG ostinato. (You can play this part with younger groups.)
- Add the unpitched ostinato to bring out the clock's mechanical character.
- Direct the chime strokes for the hour chosen by the students.

## Author's Note

Substitute your name for mine or devise a new lyric phrase for the first three beats. For example: "Central's happy student"s . . .   "Grade three students" . . .   "Mrs. Johnson's students" . . .

## Process Suggestions

- Teach the song to the class. If the students know *Shortnin' Bread,* begin there.
- Teach the new lyrics using a visual.
- Add the A section accompanying ostinatos one-at-a-time. Begin with basses.
- Add the B section xylophone solos.
- Teach the A section melody to the SX/AX players. In performance, add the SX/AX to the melody on the *D.C.*

## Extension

- Use the B section for four-measure improvisations or two-measure question/answer phrases.
- Substitute metallophones for xylophones in the lyrics and melody performance sections. You will also have to adjust the rhythm slightly to fit the lyrics.

# FRED PENTATONIC

**Barred & Unpitched Instrument Ostinatos**

arr. Konnie Saliba

## Process Suggestions
- Show how the F Pentatonic scale looks on the barred instruments and with a visual: no Bs or Es.
- Teach the melody to the class. Divide into three parts for measure eight.
- Teach the barred instrument ostinatos and add to the melody.
- Teach the unpitched ostinato and add to the arrangement.

## Extensions
- Ask students to devise a new unpitched ostinato.
- Create a speech B section containing story elaboration.

# AUSTINATO

**Vocal & Unpitched Instrument Ostinatos**

Konnie Saliba

(V) Let's go to Aus-tin, come on down. Let's go to Aus-tin to bur-ri-to town.
Let's go to Aus-tin, swing a-long. Let's sing some Aus-ti-na-tos, with our song.

(VO-1) Soft tor-til-las nice and fat. Roll them out flat they'll be read-y like that.

(VO-2) Add the sauce so mild or hot. Mmmmmm. Add the sauce, I like it hot! Mmmmmm.

(VO-3) Lots of beans, on-ions too. We make it spe-cial just for you.

## Process Suggestions

- Teach the four-bar melody, with repeat.
- Add the unpitched ostinatos.
- Prepare each vocal ostinato, with repeat.
- Then perform the melody with guitar. Add the vocal ostinatos one at a time.
- Layer the piece in different ways. For example:
    a. melody—melody with VO-1—melody with VO-1 & 2.
    b. VO-1—VO-1 & 2—VO-1, 2 & 3—VO-1, 2, & 3 (softly) plus melody.

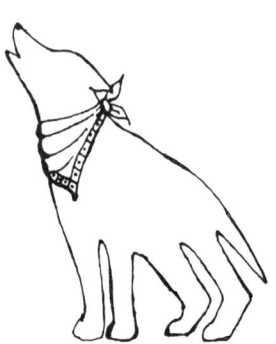

# IF YOU LIKE ME

## Author's Notes

- Vocal ostinatos are the most difficult kind to create with musicality. The similarity of children's vocal timbres, the tendency for ostinato lyrics to conflict with melody lyrics, and the tendency for short vocal ostinatos to sound insipid all contribute to the problem.
- Ostinato 1, a basic *Sol-Mi* pattern, can be enhanced by gestures of friendship to each other.
- Ostinato 2 retains the *Sol-Mi* foundation but adds one pitch plus gestures related to the lyrics.
- Longer ostinatos will be most successful when based on known musical concepts. Ostinato 3 uses the tonic triad and part of the key's scale. Ostinato 4 is based on the *I-V* interval and the *V* triad.

## Process Suggestions

- Teach the song, with gestures.
- Divide the class and add ostinato 1 **or** 2. Teach both and let students pick their favorite.
- Older students can add ostinato 3 **or** 4 to the melody.
- Advanced students can be divided into three groups: melody, ostinato 1 **or** 2, ostinato 3 **or** 4. You could also perform ostinatos 2, 3, and 4 in additive fashion.

# HOT DOG

## Process Suggestions

- Teach the melody and the ostinatos to everyone with guitar accompaniment.
- Add the unpitched percussion ostinato and perform.
- Divide the class. Sing the melody with each of the ostinatos, one at a time.
- Divide into three or four groups. Begin with the melody then layer in the ostinatos.